Give Me Liberty
Or
Give Me Death

Exposing the Deplorable
Business Practices of
Some
Florida Homeowner
Associations

By Rita Harshman

TRUE PERSPECTIVE
PUBLISHING HOUSE

Give Me Liberty or Give Me Death

Copyright ©2019 by Rita Harshman
Give me Liberty or Give Me Death
Printed in the United States of
America

ISBN 978-1-7340305-4-9

INTRODUCTION

The following is a treatise, if you will, of events I've encountered as a Florida resident who has been embroiled in a legal battle with my local Homeowner's Association. In my opinion, due to a lack of local governmental oversight, Florida Homeowner's Associations are given a proverbial license to kill; or at least a license to destroy the lives of residents who dare to challenge their unethical business practices.

I am an 87-year-old widow who has been entrenched legally in an untenable conflict with the Florida Pines Homeowner's Association and Aegis, their property managers. Moving forward I will refer to them as the HOA. I'm writing this treatise to expose them and to warn future unsuspecting Florida Homeowners as to the unscrupulous business practices that these HOA's are capable of. These true events occurred to me over a period of three years from 2016 until 2019. Florida homeowners are aware of these horror stories and live in fear of these events ever happening to them or someone they care for.

The writing style of this book is fluid, conversational and informal because I don't want any of my passion or nuances of this evil that lurks in our society to be misunderstood or understated. My prayer is that my experiences will in some way educate the unsuspecting innocent as well as encourage those who are encountering the same grief.

REMEMBER THE
ASTRONAUTS
WARNING:

"HOUSTON, WE HAVE
A PROBLEM!"

WELL….

WAKE UP AMERICA –
"WE   HAVE   A
PROBLEM."

Table of Contents

Florida Law Cracks Down on HOA Dictatorships Effective July 1, 2013

This law was legislated because of the so-called HOA Dictatorships in Florida, creating more of a structure for how HOA's are run. It is referred to a "common sense" bill. Some of the key concerns addressed include: a homeowner's right to HOA documents, HOA officers with a criminal past, HOA officers with a financial interest in certain bids and state investigation of complaints against HOA officers and managers.

Question: Is there any legal protection for homeowners?

The answer is a resounding yes. These expectations are based on rights established in the law, or on basic standards of decency and respect:

Homeowners deserve a response to an inquiry:

Homeowners should expect that HOA financial and other records will be kept in a routine manner for reasonably easy access. Homeowners should expect disclosure procedures which ensure easy access to most documents within a reasonable time and without unreasonable restrictions.

Homeowners should get a timely notice and a fair opportunity to be heard if the HOA intends to take disciplinary action against them.

By knowing what is expected of the HOA and its governing board, you can better understand where you stand in the scheme of things, and what rights you have as a member.

When both parties work together towards one common goal, it is amazing the community they can build.

Question: Why do we have Florida laws governing the HOA if we do not intend to enforce them?

The answer is section 102: The right to resolve disputes without litigation; (ii) states that homeowners and associations will have available alternative dispute resolution, although both parties preserve the right to litigate.

Give Me Liberty or Give Me Death

1. Required notice of violation… must do the following: state any amount the association claims is due, mediate the problem and solve, obtain a hearing without incurring any attorney fees charged by the association.

2. Right to a hearing, at no cost to verify facts and seek resolution. Homeowner must be allowed to appeal to the directors.

3. No lawsuit without directors voting. Must have most of all directors in compliance with applicable law and governing documents that may set super-majority vote or other requirements.

4. Exception for emergencies, which would determine homeowner rights to end conditions resulting in the

immediate and significant threat.

The law makers were "spot-on" to prohibit hiring attorneys because they would only escalate the problem and drum up fake claims in order to gain unnecessary fees and the disputes would still not be resolved.

Why cause the homeowner great damages and to suffer the bullying, harassment, threats and finally, the force, and probably end up having the homeowner evicted or thrown out of their home?

Mediation would have probably solved the issue, and all would be happy campers. History has proven that the party who refuses to mediate, is probably the one at fault. They certainly do not want the matter of their wrongdoing to come to light.

Question: Does the plaintiff not know that they have broken the law on all counts?

Question: The plaintiff is noted as Florida Pines Homeowner's Association. What happened to Aegis, the perpetrator of this fraud?

Now we have Artimis, the third Plaintiff by another name.

Motto: A crook by any other name is still a crook.

Ashley Moody, Florida Attorney General

After having considered all of the following rules and regulations regarding HOA's and homeowners relationships, I thought that I had my back covered by the #1 State's Political Ally.

Ashley Moody promised to fight fraud, and the scams they commit against Floridians. She had the perfect case presented to her and her staff. As you will see, the HOA not only harassed, bullied me, threatened me and finally, by filing an unlawful suit, forced me to pay the double-billed dues, plus the attorney's fees which were entirely false.

All the Florida State Laws were completely ignored by the HOA, and all the government established departments, which are to serve the taxpayers, have denied their responsibility towards stopping this fraud. The consumer protection division of the office of the Florida AG is a civil enforcement agency that focuses its efforts on identifying unfair and deceptive business practices. They go on to say, "our office reviews complaints to identify complex patterns of questionable business activities that effect numerous consumers in multiple judicial circuits."

They suggest I reach out to attorneys, for Florida residents aged 60 or older. I called the Florida Senior Legal Helpline, which is free. Well, they turned me down because they considered me too well- off since I own my home free and clear, and I have income from social security and a small pension from Lockheed Martin.

The Department of Business & Professional Regulation, "DBPR", plus the many lawyers and realtors that I have talked to, all want their hourly rate paid before even speaking to me. In other words, unless you are willing to pay, no deal.

The State of Florida plays the same game as our Federal Government in Washington, D.C. "Keep kicking the can down the road because the pay is good."

Give Me Liberty or Give Me Death

So, what about our Constitution (signed by my forefather, Caesar Rodney, delegate representing the State of Delaware), which states, "with liberty and justice for all."

He had to be carried into Independence Hall in Philadelphia on a stretcher because he was sick and dying, but he was a loyal and responsible American, and he knew that he must sign that document.

I cannot let him down.

I was only eight years old in 1940, when WWII was raging across the pond. There was a large poster of Uncle Sam which was featured on all the post offices and government buildings showing him pointing his finger at me, (yes, I thought he was pointing at me), and he was saying to me, "Be all you can be." He changed my life. The war was the truth, the whole truth, and nothing but the truth.

Give Me Liberty or Give Me Death

If the preceding HOA information sounds familiar to you, or if a similar situation happened to you, or if you just decided to cave in and pay, then read my story. This will curl your hair.

I sold my home in Orlando, which my husband and I purchased in December of 1959. We lived there for a total of 56 years, raised our two sons there, and I considered this house my husband's castle.

He repaired, built, added on, painted inside and out, and he took care of the yard which was his life-saving hobby. I used to think he loved the house more than me, but of course, that was nonsense.

He passed away in February of 2005, and I remained there until our two sons considered it was time for me to find a new life, only because the memories

were too strong and heart-breaking. It was pay-back time for the boys, they took charge and with loving care and concern, let me find my own way to a new home, in Clermont, Florida,
where there are so many neighbors in the same life struggle and providing to me all the necessary strength and will power to continue on. God bless them all.

No matter what life has to offer at the moment, count your blessings. It could be worse. What would my life be like if I were Jewish and living in Germany in 1940?

A New Home for My Youngest Son

January 22, 2016 – My youngest son Norman, and I ventured out on many occasions to find a home not too far from Clermont, where I now live. He could not move in with me as Kings Ridge is a senior neighborhood, and you must be over 55 years old to reside here. Who wants to live with their mother anyway? We found a very nice house, just the size he was looking for, and the price was right.

Give Me Liberty or Give Me Death

We purchased the house on 22nd of January of 2016 and paid for the house in full. At closing, we were told that the neighborhood had an HOA and we were to pay the prorated amount for January, and the total amount due for February and March. I agreed to that, because I had two HOA's for Kings Ridge, one for the golf courses, the club houses, pools, tennis courts, etc.

The other HOA was for the district where my home was located, and they took care of the irrigation of my lawn, mowing, edging, insect control, fertilizing the grass, and many other duties and responsibilities thereof. At my age, I considered this a Godsend. I thought this was great news for Norm also because he is not a yard person and would not keep up the appearances which were expected in such a clean and well-ordered neighborhood.

Give Me Liberty or Give Me Death

We received the payment booklet for the next quarter, for April, May and June, due April 1st and I paid the $435.00 on April 12, ck#506, which cleared my bank.

I like to pay my bills on time, and I pay by check. I do not trust the banks to pay for me. The 2nd payment paid for $435.00, ck#521, for July, cleared my bank 8-8-2016. This is when I decided to write my own checks and mail them myself.

I received a letter from HOA showing overdue balance of $435, however, that check had already cleared my bank. The 3rd payment for October was paid $435.00, ck#525, cleared my bank on 10-4-2016; so much for the first year of Florida Pines HOA.

Give Me Liberty or Give Me Death

The AEGIS Property Manager

On January 2, 2017, I received the payment coupon book for the quarterly payments. The amount due was the same, so I paid the $435.00 by ck#8574 dated January 2, 2017, hoping that we would finally be on the right track. As I said, I like to pay my bills on time, and keep on the right track. The payment was paid to Florida Pines HOA at P.O. Box 628207, Orlando FL, which was the same address as the previous year.

Give Me Liberty or Give Me Death

The 2nd payment booklet was received February 1, 2017. Since I already paid for the 1st quarterly payment, Jan, Feb, Mar., I did not understand why I was receiving a different booklet beginning February, and the mailing address was c/o Aegis CMS, P.O. Box 64203, in Phoenix, Az. 85082.

A little late, but better late than never, I received a letter from David Burman, AMS R CAM, as President of Aegis, informing me that Aegis was engaged as Community Management Solutions, Inc, He also informs me that my account is $435.00 in arears. I called the phone number as provided, 863-256-#### to let him know that my account was paid in full through Jan, Feb. and March, of 2017, and that all payments had cleared my bank. I had asked that a corrected payment booklet be supplied to me so that I would not be paying double. I also was leery that the payments were to be paid to Phoenix instead of locally. It made no sense to me that I should be paying a HOA fee to someone located in Phoenix.

They were not very nice to me, yelling that I cannot call, I must write if I have any problems. That put real doubts in my mind that this whole Aegis thing was a scam.

As time went by, a strange thing happened, my in- house water bill, which was always in the price range of $45.00 to $55.00 per month, skyrocketed to over $100.00 above the normal monthly rate. This went on for many months. I asked Norm if he had drained his pool, then refilled it, and he replied that he had not. Overages started in June 2016 and continued until April of 2018.

I wrote a letter to both Polk Utilities and to Aegis on the same letter, letting them know of this problem, and only Polk Utilities responded and, upon their inspection, implied that someone had tampered with the water meter located on the side of my house. I have their letter letting me know that they did not reset the water meter. I then had to turn off the water meter since the HOA did not confirm the resetting for irrigation and they would not correct their double billing mistake. When I asked them about the use for irrigation, they told me that they did not use the water for irrigation. Why then does their yearly budget show irrigation fees and maintenance fees?

Needless to say, I smelled a rat.

For the rest of 2017, I received dunning letters letting me know that I was behind, and I let them know that I was still waiting for the corrected booklet. If they could take the time to send me letters telling me I am behind in my payments, they could likewise take the time to correct their mistake of double billing. I also noticed that their mail to me was from an address at 2 Jungle Hut Rd – Suite 1, Palm Coast, FL 32137. How come the payments go to Phoenix?

Now I know this is a set-up. I let them know that if they would correct their mistake, I will pay my dues. The problem would be solved.

Never once have I ever implied that I would not pay the dues. However, I will still need to have the coupon booklet corrected. I even sent them an email stating that I could and would show them a legal way to solve this problem by sending me a letter acknowledging their mistake and by using that letter, I could use the incorrect payment booklet using their letter with their approval to change the due dates on the booklet pages.

Give Me Liberty or Give Me Death

There are simple ways to solve problems, and those who do not want to solve the simple problems, have their reasons to not do so. This was not a mistake, this was done with malice of forethought, to obtain illegal rights and funds.

If you can come up with another answer, I would love to hear from you.

The Supposed Purpose
of
Homeowner Associations

I truly believed that we as the homeowners decided to hire these associations to keep our neighborhoods looking good, upper class clean, orderly and above all, friendly. There were to be no chicken coops built in back yards to raise chickens; no teenage band practicing in garages to all hours of the night, no loud music, or other disturbing noises till all hours of the night, and no pets running wild all over the neighborhood making it impossible to take a walk.

There are rules of what not to do, and rules to make sure you do this or that for the benefit of all who live there. However, all problems can be addressed and solved to everyone's satisfaction without yelling, screaming, or going to court. It is called mediation, which is law.

To me, this would be like my marriage. I lived fifty-five years with my husband, who was a Marine and who was also an American Space Scientist. Believe me, it was like "putting the flag up on Iwo Jima" but you never could say, "I won't, or I can't" to a Marine. This was the basis of our solid marriage, to mediate or talk things out to a peaceful solution.

2018 – A Year of Infamy

On January 1, 2018, I received a delinquency notice from Florida Pines HOA and you guessed it, the address was 2 Jungle Hut Rd., Suite 1, Palm Coast, FL 32137. They state that the amount due is $1,768.02. They are still not acknowledging that the first quarter payment was paid in 2017. They sure are a mixed-up management company when they cannot get their bookkeeping straight. But here is the best part. The letter is not signed by anyone, just Florida Pines, HOA, Inc. What happened to Aegis, the managing company?

They still do not give me credit for the first quarter paid. They say I owe $1,768.02, when I really owe $1,305.00. They remind me that this is an action to collect a debt. I reminded them again, that I still have not received their corrected invoice.

Another letter was received from Rodney Cotton, and he also has misquoted what amount was due and owing. At this point in time, they are an entire year behind in correcting their invoice, and I should not be billed for interest due for non-payment of their error.

According to every lawyer I know regarding contracts or invoices, that are incorrect, if you pay it, you are admitting that you agree. You will be very sorry for letting them get the better of their mistake, and you will never regain that payment that you made in error. This is how scam artists get away with their deceit.

Also, keep in mind that senior citizens are fair game and are targeted because they either do not know what to do, or figure it is more trouble than all the misery they will experience by harassment, bullying, threats and force. This is their M.O. (method of operation). Just check out the Better Business Bureau and see all the cases they have against Aegis, and, I might add, doing the exact type of fraud.

In my opinion, I have concluded that the reason Aegis is not the entity suing me, but Florida Pines, who probably is hiding behind some rock, because they have done this before and now it is Aegis's turn. Next, we now have our third HOA, Artimis, who will continue to take aim at the victim and be the cover- up for Florida Pines and Aegis. Where does it all end?

Give Me Liberty or Give Me Death

Remember the 2013 Florida law which states that mediation should be offered to solve disputes, and without litigation.

On January 16, 2018, I receive some payment stubs, which were just pieces of paper, showing 1-1-2017 for payment of $435.00, which as I have said many times that it was paid but again it was a year late, and still shows Phoenix as the address. There are also stubs for 4-1-2017, 7-1-2017 for $435.00, and 10-1-2017 for $435.00, all not paid because I am now positive this is a scam.

Why would I say that? Because I also received a payment booklet starting 1-1-2018, and the payment amount is for $420.00 for the entire year of 2018. They crossed out the other quarterly coupons. The payment address is still located in Phoenix, however, the office address for Florida Pines and Aegis is local, at 8390 Champions Gate Blvd.

304, Champions Gate FL 33896. What is going on here?

Something is amiss. I receive an email from Polk County Irrigation Inspections and another notice informing the residents that all maintenance and landscaping services on the "short term" lots will end on December 31, 2017. I am not a short-term lot owner.

That leaves me with one last question, why do they not correctly bill me, and I will pay what is due and owing? Can they not accept that they made an error, whether by accident, or by intent, to solve the problem that they have created?

The answer to my question is, "It was not a mistake." This double-billed coupon was done with knowledge, and malice of fore-thought.

Give Me Liberty or Give Me Death

Which reminds me, (the victim and homeowner), that crooks are smarter than ordinary folks. We old seniors do not want trouble in our old age, so pay it.

Only problem with that, they will do it repeatedly if allowed to get away with it. Just think about that.

If you do let them get away with this fraud, you are aiding and abetting their crime. I remind you again, that our legal help told me to get a lawyer. I did. Her name is Ashley Moody, and she's the best for this job. You promised, AG Moody, now deliver.

2019 Litigation Begins

March 3, 2018, I received a letter from Rodney Cotton, of Aegis, advising me not to call or leave a voice message. I must write, and he is telling me for the final time that I must make a payment in the amount of $1,782.69. Why is it, that when I write to them, they never answer my letter, or correct the invoice which shows the over-payment? I ask again for a meeting to solve this problem and was denied.

Since they do not correct their over-billing, what am I supposed to do?

Give Me Liberty or Give Me Death

On March 22, 2018, I received a coupon book with four quarterly payments for 2018. The entire year was approved with every owner paying only $420.00 and we were to destroy the remaining coupons. So, now my question is: "What does the $420.00 pay for in services for the entire year?"

I ask Aegis again for a meeting to settle this agreement, once and for all. You write that I can go on the website to find the answers to all my questions. Since I am 87 years old, and do not have all the abilities to go online and do all the things that other folks do, wouldn't it have been gracious of them to respect me, and get it over with on agreeable terms that we both can relate to.

All I ask of the association and Aegis, was to correct their over-billing. That was too much to ask for, so what did they do? They did the one thing that was against the Florida State rules governing homeowners' associations, they filed a claim against me for their error and fraud.

On May 16, 2018, I received the Ruggieri Law Firm letter stating that I owe $1,797.49, and with the added attorney's fees for a total of $2,095.71. Now the HOA and their attorney (debt collector) have still not corrected the over-billing and threatening has now been added to the damages suffered by me, the homeowner, because of their scam and fraud.

I do not waste any time in my responses, I wrote my letter on May 19, 2018, to Aegis, Attn: David l. Burman, as President, of Aegis Community Management Solutions, Inc. I let him know that their mistake has not yet been corrected.

What else is new? So many times, I requested an explanation of the irrigation problem between Polk Water and Aegis. As Rodney said in his letter, my son, Norman, tried to explain to me what he thought happened.

Norman is not, and still is not, aware of who was to blame, and that same condition continued for months, until we had to take the matter in our hands, and we turned off the irrigation water meter from inside our home. The Polk Water Utilities stated in their letter that the meter had been tampered with prior to our blocking the irrigation.

We know who it did, a neighbor saw and described the person tampering with our meter and said that the same person was seen tampering with their meter. I know from experience, that this is considered hearsay, but nevertheless, I know they saw what they saw, and said what they saw.

The longer that time goes by on these cases, I fully understand why the

Give Me Liberty or Give Me Death

Florida Law effective July 1, 2010, clearly states: "This provision does not protect the welfare of the communities or the owners; it protects the income of the attorneys and the assets of the banks to the detriment of owners and associations." The attorneys made sure that they would get paid first – and only the remaining money, if any, will go to the association. This law goes on the say:

"These guidelines make sure that homeowners will be protected against unreasonable collection costs, but still allows them to go after the "deadbeats."

On May 31, 2018, I receive a letter from Bekki Tyler. She takes the word of Rodney Cotton, of Aegis, but never once considers all the facts of why this fraud has been allowed to continue.

Four attempts using the same letter to solve this problem with the law firm have gotten nowhere. Every time I wrote, I sent the same letter, asking for a meeting to solve this, once and for all. But never received an invitation to meet to negotiate terms. Why? Because the perpetrators of crimes do not want to negotiate, since the facts will show that they are the reason for the crime in the first place.

When I worked at a law firm, in order to accept a case against the defendant, we did what was called "due-diligence." we wanted to make sure that we were not defending criminals, crooks, and thieves.

The dictionary definition says that due diligence is "the care that a reasonable person exercises to avoid harm to other persons or their property." In plain English, due diligence means doing your homework.

On June 7, 2018, I sent off another letter to Frank Ruggieri, regarding intent to record a claim of lien. Please note that I have again requested mediation between Aegis and me.

July 20, 2018 – second request – same letter.

October 25, 2018 – third request – same letter.

Summons – this was filed 10-19-2018, but I did not receive this until 11-13-2018.

Notice of Lis Pendens – this was also filed 10-19-2018 but delivered to me on 11-13-2018. They are in a big hurry to file these claims to get their fees. They have no intention to settle, nor have they ever intended to settle.

Foreclosure Complaint – same circumstances, no intention to settle. They want whatever they can get.

Summons – personal service on an individual – please note that I had to hand-deliver my response because there was no case number on the summons. I went to the court, and the clerk provided to me a Case No. 2018-CA-004179. So now you can understand why I know this is all a scam, set up to obtain whatever they can get in fees, and maybe even my home.

Notice of dropping parties – unknown spouse of Rita Harshman. They knew, or should have known, that I am widowed, my husband of 55 years passed away February 22, 2005.

2019 – You guessed it; we are still at it.

January 1, 2019 – I received the coupon book for 2019 and again we are only required to pay the one fee for $420.00 for the entire year. If they had any respect for the homeowners they work for, they would agree to mediate any problem, and agree to possibly a monthly payment of $35.00 per month.

Think about this for one minute; who else pays for services to be rendered for an entire year, without knowing what they are paying for? And The one-time payment is to be made to Aegis in Phoenix, Az. What happened to Artimis, who represents Florida Pines Homeowners Association, Inc., and their address is 8390 Champions Gate Blvd., suite 304, Champions Gate, FL 33896.

I remind myself again - a crook by any other name, is still a crook.

I have several pleadings from the law firm regarding the "unknown" tenant. There is no "unknown" tenant. I own the home, and my son lives there. He does not pay rent, electricity, water, or phone bills. I am not a liar, I do not represent this home as my principal residence, and therefore, I pay full property taxes, I do not file homestead exemption. My principal residence is in Clermont, Florida, and I claim Homestead Exemption for this property only.

Filing all these "unknown" tenant default claims, motions, etc. is the precise reason the Florida laws governing homeowners concludes that all the disputes can be, and should be, settled out of court. There are so many false and unnecessary court filings that it is a complete joke, but they can claim court costs and attorney fees? Money is the root of all evil.

The attorney firm hired to represent the HOA also had me sign the settlement without the proper documentation, by the notary public, which requires that I sign before the notary and present my identification proving that I am the person who signed. The notary was not present, asking for the required identification.

I received an amended notice of hearing (15 minutes reserved) scheduled for February 27th, 2019.
I was judged guilty before I set foot in the court room. I attended this hearing with my two sons, Hal and Jose, because I cannot drive and have age related physical problems. The hearing was a disaster. I was not allowed to present any proof of what this case is all about and would prove to the court that this case was a scam perpetrated by them to gain unlawful rights and money. The HOA violated every State Law which governs HOA's and their relationship with the homeowners who they represent. I still do not get it!

The Ruggieri law firm provided a Motion to Approve Settlement, which was entirely made up by them, with no mediation or arbitration on my part.

Give Me Liberty or Give Me Death

They were in a hurry to get me to sign the settlement, or have my home put up for auction by force. I had to either pay up or lose my home. I had to travel to their office to sign the papers in order to stop the sale.

I recall in the movie scenes, where the bad guys put a noose, hanging from a tree, around my neck, put me on a horse, and then demand that I do as I am told, or else. If not, they swat the horse on the rear, and I am left hanging to die. Well, there was no John Wayne to save me, so I had to pay. Funny? Well, this was reality. No attorney was willing to help me because I had no funds, I had already been taken for all my available cash by a law firm, who did, in fact, have the Staples/Wells Fargo lawsuit dismissed with prejudice.

Seniors vs. Crime interviewed me, look notes, but there again, did not examine the documents I had, and I have not heard from them since.

The DBPR is also too busy, or I am not eligible for their services. I guess that I must be an illegal or destitute to obtain the help from my government services, for which I pay for.

Homeowners associations sure know how to play the game, their M.O. (method of operation) is, "we got away with it before, and we can do it again." They sure know how to get what they want.

What did Yogi Berra say? "It ain't over 'till it's over."

By just reading the foregoing, anyone should deem that this is a criminal case, and it must be stopped. They have done this before. You don't believe me? Then check out the Better Business Bureau, and then you will believe that they will do it again. It is up to you, my dear reader, to help me stop this unlawful, well-planned fraud. I will fight to the end, but I will play fair.

The Summary Final Judgment, stating that my home will be sold at auction on May 2nd, 2019, is a complete and total disgrace. As a decent American, and law-abiding citizen, I could not, and would not, allow myself to stoop so low as to take a home from anyone because they demanded that a scam operation be stopped.

I ask myself this, how would that judge feel if I was willing to throw his mother, or grandmother, out of their home because they sought truth and justice, and their rights as an American, tax-paying citizen? Whatever happened to our Pledge to the Flag of the United States of America? "With liberty and justice for all."

Give Me Liberty or Give Me Death

Florida law prohibits filing a lawsuit, other than for emergency circumstances.

I mailed to the court, a Second Request in Answer to Notice of Hearing, dated April 23, 2019, and I did not hear from them. I called the clerk of the court to inquire whether the pleading was received by certified mail, and I was told that they did not receive it. Please note the address as Polk County Courthouse, Civil Division.

The clerk gave me the phone number of Judge Hill's office, and I called immediately, I did not want my home sold at auction because of their lame excuse that the second request was not received by them, again. When I was talking to the clerk, I held in my hand the return receipt, which was signed and dated April 26, 2019.

Give Me Liberty or Give Me Death

Original return receipt which was received by the court dated 4/26/19.

They want my home, and they will do all or anything to get it.

Remember Attorney Cohen, crying into the TV camera, that he was convicted and now he must go to jail serving several years, and he has a wife and family. He thought he would get away with his deceit and all because he lied under oath.

Remember when I stated that the homeowner's associations rule by harassment, bullying, threats and finally, with force. I was right. Read on:

This Ruggieri law firm, was only interested in filing for attorney fees, they were not seeking truth and justice under the laws of the State of Florida.

Give Me Liberty or Give Me Death

I had filed four of the identical letters to this law firm who identifies themselves as debt collectors. They were never interested in settlement of this case. This also confirms the cause of this complaint, which was instigated by Aegis to create a scam, and to hopefully terrify the old lady who owns the home. They have the standard operating procedure down to a science, and were successful many times, so why not go for it again.

January 2, 2019, a default was entered by Stacy Butterfield, Clerk of the Circuit Court, because the defendant, unknown tenant, failed to serve or file a paper as required by law. There is no unknown tenant. So how much did the debt collector charge for this unnecessary filing?

January 17, 2019, Motion for Summary Final Judgment and to tax attorneys' fees and costs was filed. They still insist that the owner failed to pay assessments, including the 1ˢᵗ quarter fees. How many times must I remind them that the first quarter of 2017 was paid in full, and my bank account clearly shows that it was paid, and the fee cleared my bank account. This is just another way for the debt collector to collect fees under illegal greedy circumstances.

January 17, 2019, an Affidavit of Non-compliance and Indebtedness, was filed by the association manager, Gabby, which shows that the 1ˢᵗ quarter has no balance forward, so how does the so-called debt collector's fees not coincide with the homeowner's fees that are due and owing?

January 17, 2019, another Attorney's Affidavit as to costs was filed. This affidavit shows all title search, filing fee, service of process, recording, copies, and total. They sure are racking up costs as fast as possible, but never doing a "due diligence" to confirm if this is a legal lawsuit under the law. I guess that they forgot to check to see if under Florida law, they can file a lawsuit under the illegal practices of this homeowner's association. The law governing litigation clearly states that the citizen property owner is not liable to pay any court costs or attorney fees. REALLY?

As the Defendant, I had to file Answer to Notice of Hearing to gather all necessary information to provide to the court why this judgment must be reconsidered because of false or misinformation given to the court for said hearing. I was not granted a hearing.

March 18, 2019, Summary Final Judgment was signed by Gerald P. Hill, II, and the court awards reasonable attorney's fees of $2,550.00. This judgment also states that the court shall sell the property at public sale on May 2nd, 2019. This judge must not know what the Florida Law says, that all disputes must be settled by arbitration, and no lawsuit should ever be initiated.

In my opinion, this judge is guilty of obstruction of justice and aiding and abetting a crime.

Read the Florida Law – and using common sense, what one must do if one makes a mistake, is to admit it, say you are sorry, and then commence to correct this terrible injustice.

I might add, my common sense also tells me, "Never do unto others what you would not want them to do unto you."

March 1, 2019 – The Plot Thickens

Another attorney fees affidavit entitled Amended Attorney's Affidavit of Actual fees, was submitted to the court and signed by Anthony T. Paris III, and notarized, shows a list of costs incurred totaling $3,650.00. This affidavit was a complete farce.

First, they did not attend the so-called hearing. I was present and had to be driven there because I am unable to drive due to physical ailments. I always conformed to the court's ruling. Please note that I have never said I would not pay the proper dues. I only demanded that they correct their false billing, which they did not do, and as of this date, have not done. Again, I replied by letter to this debt collector, that I am willing to settle this problem and I would be willing to meet at their convenience to arbitrate.

I never heard back from them. Does that sound familiar? I never heard back from Florida Pines, or Aegis concerning settlement either. Of course, settlement means that we meet, come to a fair and just agreement, shake hands, and go on with our lives. However, that would not feather their nests with ill-gotten gains.

Oh yes, money is the root of all evil. Therefore, Florida Law prohibits filing a lawsuit, other than for emergency circumstances.

Give Me Liberty or Give Me Death

I mailed to the court, the following Second Request in Answer to Notice of Hearing, dated April 23, 2019, and I did not hear from them. I called the clerk of the court to inquire whether the pleading was received by certified mail, and I was told that they did not receive it. Please note the address as Polk County Courthouse, Civil Division.

The clerk gave me the phone number of Judge Hill's office, and I called immediately. I did not want my home sold at auction because of their lame excuse that the second request was not received by them again.

Give Me Liberty or Give Me Death

Attached hereto is the payment coupon, return receipt and cancelled check which was received by the court dated 4/26/19.

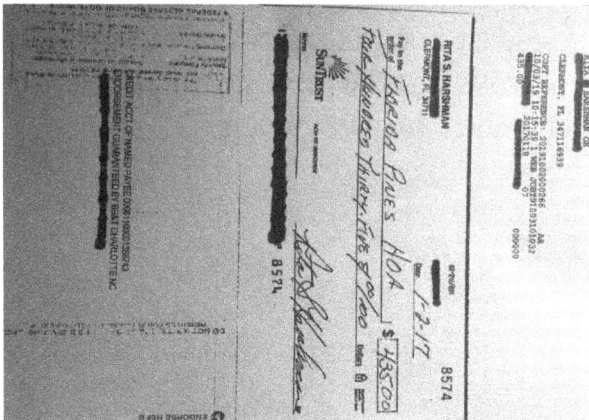

They want my home, and they will do all or anything to get it.

The Pledge of Allegiance to Our Flag

I pledge allegiance to the flag of the United States of America and to the republic for which it stands. One nation, under God, indivisible with liberty and justice for all.

Question?

Do our courts, who work for the people, and paid for by the people, maintain these standards when they judge in a court of law?

When a final judgment is wrongfully proclaimed, by a judge, who did not, and would not consider the facts, does this not make you wonder?

What is happening in our country?

Damages and the Unintended Consequences

As I write this foregoing log of facts, I think about what I had to do to save my home:

The time I had to spend asking for a ride to the court or to the attorney's office. I recall the various attorneys who would not take this case because of fees, and there were many. I think of the physical and mental problems brought on because of the stress and sleepless nights.

Give Me Liberty or Give Me Death

My income has been greatly exceeded by the financial liabilities outgo. The worst part of all this is a very sad fact: How am I and my son, going to continue to live in a neighborhood governed by evil, deceitful people who will stoop to no end to commit fraud, to win a case which should have never been brought to court in the first place?

I have always lived in peace and harmony with my neighbors, and I had hoped that my son would live there happily ever after.

Finally, because I am 87 years, they have taken away from me, my golden years.

What does all the above amount to in dollars and cents? I cannot put a price on them; I have only one life to live, and that life I will live to the best of my ability.

My Prayer:

**In all my trials, great or small,
my confidence shall be, unshaken,
as I cry dear Lord, I place my trust
in thee.**

**And when I say my prayers every
night, I ask God, "why me, Lord?"
He always responds, "I am not done
with you yet, you have a job to do."**

Amen!

Give Me Liberty or Give Me Death

www.ingramcontent.com/pod-product-compliance
Lightning Source LLC
Chambersburg PA
CBHW032017190326
41520CB00007B/509